The Story of THE CLASH

Volume 1

© 1992 EMI Virgin Music Ltd
International Music Publications Ltd
Southend Road, Woodford Green, Essex IG8 8HN, England

Music arranged and transcribed by Barnes Music Engraving Ltd

CONTENTS

THE MAGNIFICENT SEVEN

Words & Music by
The Clash

The mag - ni - fi - cent sev-en. Ring, ring. It's sev-en A. M.

Move y' - self__ to go a - gain.__ Cold wa - ter in the face__

brings you back__ to this aw - ful place. Knuck-le mer - chants and you bank - ers too,

must get up__ an' learn those rules. Weath-er - man__ and the cra - zy chief,

one says sun and one says sleet. A. M. the F. M. the P. M. too,__

churn - ing out__ that boo - ga - loo. Gets you up__ and gets you out.

But how long__ can you keep it up? Gim - me Hon - da. Gim - me So - ny.

So cheap and real pho - ny. Hong Kong dol-lars and In - di - an cents,

Eng - lish pounds and Es - ki - mo pence. You lot. What?

Don't stop. Give it all you got. You lot. What? Don't stop. You lot. What?

Don't stop. Give it all you got. You lot. What? Don't stop.

continues

Working for a rise, better my station.
Take my baby to sophistication.
She's seen the ads. She thinks it's nice.
Better work hard, I seen the price.
Never mind that. It's time for the bus.
We got to work an' you're one of us.
Clocks go slow in a place of work.
Minutes drag and the hours jerk.

'When can I tell 'em wot I do?'
'In a second maaan.'
'O right, Chuck.'
Wave bub-bub-bub-bye to the boss.
It's our profit. It's his loss.
But anyway lunch bells ring.
Take one hour and do your thang.
Cheese boiger!

What do we have for entertainment?
Cops kickin' gypsies on the pavement.
Now the news: (snap to attention)
The lunar landing of the dentist convention,
Italian mobster shoots a lobster,
Seafood restaurant gets out of hand.
Wanna car in the fridge or a fridge in the car
Like cowboys do in TV land?

You lot.
What?
Don't stop.
Give it all you got.
You lot.
What?
Don't stop.

So, get back to work an' sweat some more.
The sun will sink and we'll get out the door.
It's no good for man to work in cages.
Hits the town. He drinks his wages.
You're frettin'. You're sweatin'.
But did you notice you ain't gettin'?
You're frettin'. You're sweatin'.
But did you notice you're not gettin' anywhere?
Don't you ever stop long enough to start
To get your car outta that gear?
Don't you ever stop long enough to start
To get your car outta that gear?
Karlo Marx and Frederich Engels
Came to the checkout at the 7-11.
Marx was skint but he had sense.
Engels lent him the necessary pence.

What have we got?
Yeah. What have we got?
Yeah. What have we got?
Magnificence!
What have we got?
Luther King and Mahatma Gandhi
Went to the park to check on the game,
But they was murdered by the other team
Who went on to win fifty-nil.
You can be true. You can be false.
You be given the same reward.
Socrates and Milhous Nixon
Both went the same way, through the kitchen.
Plato the Greek or Rin-Tin-Tin,
Who's more famous to the billion millions?
News flash!
Vacuum cleaner sucks up Budgie.
Ooh, no! Bub-bye.

4

ROCK THE CASBAH

Words & Music by
The Clash

to dig this chant-ing thing.   But as the wind changed di-rec-tion   and the

tem-ple band took five,   the crowd caught a whiff   of that cra-zy Cas-bah   jive.   Sha -

- reef don't like it.   Rock-in' the Cas-bah.   Rock the Cas-bah. Sha - reef don't like it.

CODA

D.%% al Coda   *D.%%*

Rock-in' the Cas-bah.   Rock   the Cas-bah. 3. The   Rock   the Cas-bah. Sha-

2. By order of the prophet,
    We ban the boogie sound.
    Degenerate the faithful
    With that crazy Casbah sound.
    But the Bedouin, they brought out the electric camel drum.
    The local guitar picker got his guitar picking thumb.
    As soon as the shareef had cleared the square,
    They began to wail:

    Shareef don't like it.
    Rockin' the Casbah.
    Rock the Casbah.
    Shareef don't like it.
    Rockin' the Casbah.
    Rock the Casbah.

3. The king called up his jet fighters,
    He said, you better earn your pay.
    Drop your bombs between the minarets
    Down the Casbah way.
    As soon as the shareef was chauffered outta there,
    The jet pilots tuned to the cockpit radio blare.
    As soon as a shareef was outta their hair,
    The jet pilots wailed:

    Shareef don't like it.
    Rockin' the Casbah.
    Rock the Casbah.
    Shareef don't like it.
    Rockin' the Casbah.
    Rock the Casbah.

THIS IS RADIO CLASH

Words & Music by
The Clash

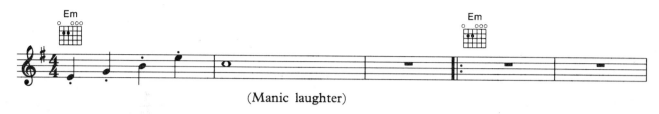

(Manic laughter)

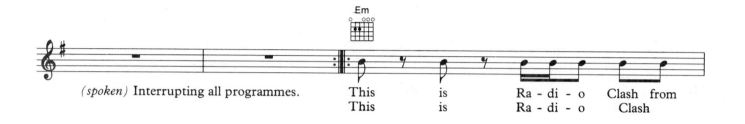

(spoken) Interrupting all programmes.

This is Ra - di - o Clash from
This is Ra - di - o Clash

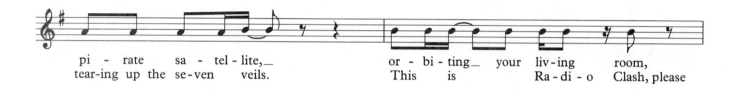

pi - rate sa - tel - lite,___ or - bi - ting___ your liv - ing room,
tear-ing up the se - ven veils. This is Ra - di - o Clash, please

cash-ing in the Bill of Rights. Cu - ban ar - my sur - plus or re -
save us, not the whales. This is Ra - di - o Clash,

-fus - ing all third lights, this is Ra - di - o Clash on
un - der-neath a mush-room cloud. This is Ra - di - o Clash, you don't

pi - rate sa - tel-lite.___ Yeah! ~
need that fun - eral shroud.

© 1981 Nineden Ltd. / Virgin Music (Publishers) Ltd.
328 Kensal Road, London W10 5XJ

This sand does not sub-scribe to the
For - ces have been

in - ter - na - tio-nal plan, in the psy-cho sha-dow of the white right hand.
loot - ing_____ my hu - ma - ni - ty._____

Them that see ghet-to - ol - o - gy___ as an ur - ban Vi - et - nam,_ the
Cur - fews have been curb - ing_____

giv-ing dead - ly ex - hi - bi - tions of mur - der by na - palm.
end of li - ber - ty._____

Oh! Oh!

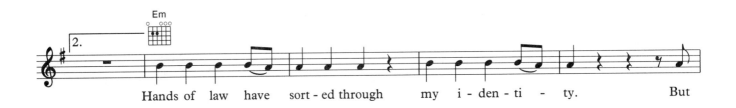

Hands of law have sort - ed through my i - den - ti - ty. But

8

now this soul is brave and wants to be free,_____

a-ny way to be free.

Em

This is Ra-di-o Clash on pi-rate sa-tel-lite.
This is not free Eur - ope

nor an armed force_ net - work.

This is Ra - di - o Clash us -ing au - dio am - mu - ni - tion.

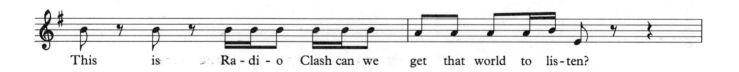

This is Ra - di - o Clash can we get that world to lis -ten?

This is Ra - di - o Clash us -ing au - ral am - mu - ni -tion.

This   is   Ra - di - o Clash can we get that world to lis -ten?

This   is   Ra - di - o Clash on pi - rate sa - tel - lite,__

or - bit - ing__ your liv -ing   room,   cash-ing in the Bill of   Rights.

This   is   Ra - di - o Clash on pi - rate sa - tel - lite.__

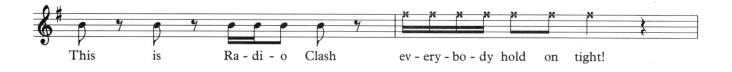

This   is   Ra - di - o Clash   ev - ery - bo - dy hold   on tight!

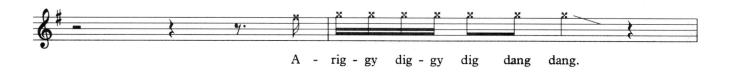

A - rig - gy dig - gy dig dang dang.

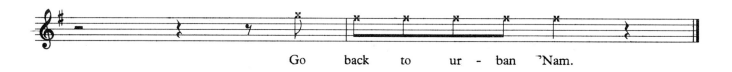

Go   back   to   ur - ban 'Nam.

STRAIGHT TO HELL

Words & Music by
The Clash

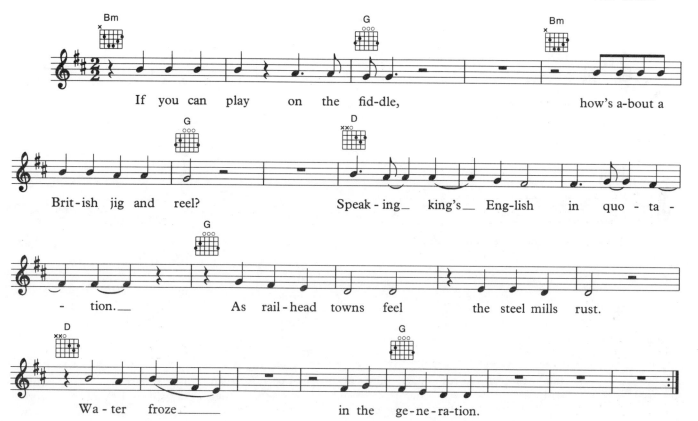

If you can play on the fid-dle, how's a-bout a Brit-ish jig and reel? Speak-ing_ king's_ Eng-lish in quo-ta--tion._ As rail-head towns feel the steel mills rust. Wa-ter froze_____ in the ge-ne-ra-tion.

2. Clear as winter ice,
This is your paradise.
There ain't no need for ya.
There ain't no need for ya.
Go straight to hell, boys.
Go straight to hell, boys.

3. Y'wanna join in a chorus
Of the Amerasian blues?
When it's Christmas out in Ho Chi Minh City,
Kiddie say Poppa Poppa Poppa Poppa Poppa San,
Take me home.
See me got photo photo photograph of you and
Mamma Mamma Mamma San,
Of you and Mamma Mamma Mamma San.

4. Lemme tell ya 'bout your blood bamboo kid.
It ain't Coca-Cola. It's rice.
Straight to hell, boys.
Go straight to hell, boys.
Go straight to hell, boys.
Go straight to hell, boys.

5. Oh Poppa San, please take me home.
Oh Poppa San, everybody, they wanna go home.
So Mamma San sez ...
(instrumental)

6. You wanna play mind crazed banjo
On the druggy-drag ragtime U.S.A.?
In Parkland International. Hah!
Junkiedom U.S.A.
Where procaine proves the purest rock man groove,
And rat poison. The volatile Molotov says ...

7. Can you cough it up loud and strong?
The immigrants,
They wanna sing all night long.
It could be anywhere.
Most likely, could be any frontier,
Any hemisphere.
No man's land.
(instrumental)

8. There ain't no asylum here.
King Solomon, he never lived round here.
Straight to hell, boys.
Go straight to hell, boys.
Go straight to hell, boys.
Go straight to hell, boys.

CLAMPDOWN

Words & Music by
Strummer/Jones

One two three four.

What are we gon - na do now?   Tak-

- ing off his tur - ban they said   is this man a Jew   work-
__ said five to ten but I said   dou - ble that a - gain. I'm not   work-
you grow up   and   you calm down,__   work-

- ing for the clamp-down.   They__ put up a pos - ter say - ing
- ing for the clamp-down.   No__ man born__ with a
- ing for the clamp-down.   You__ start wear - ing

'We earn more than you!'   We're work   - ing for the clamp - down.
liv - ing soul__ can be work   - ing for the clamp - down.
blue and brown__ and work   - ing for the clamp - down.

We will teach__ our twis - ted speech__   to__
Kick o - ver the wall,__ 'cause gov - ern - ment's to fall.   How__
So you got__ some - one__ to boss__ a - round.   It makes

the young be - lie - vers.
can we re - fuse it?
you feel big now.
We will train__ our blue__ eyed men__
Let fu - ry have the hour, an -
You drift__ un - til__ you bru -

to Coda ⊕

- ger can be power,
- tal - ize,__ you

to__ be young be - lie - vers.
made__ your first kill now.
d'you know that you can use it.

1. | 2.

The judge   The voi - ces in__ your head__ are call - ing. Stop

wast - ing your time. There's noth - ing com - ing. On - ly a fool__ would

think some-one__ could save__ you.   The men at the fac - tory are old__

__ and cun - ning. You don't owe noth - ing, so boy get run - ning. It's the

best years of__ your life__ they want to steal.__

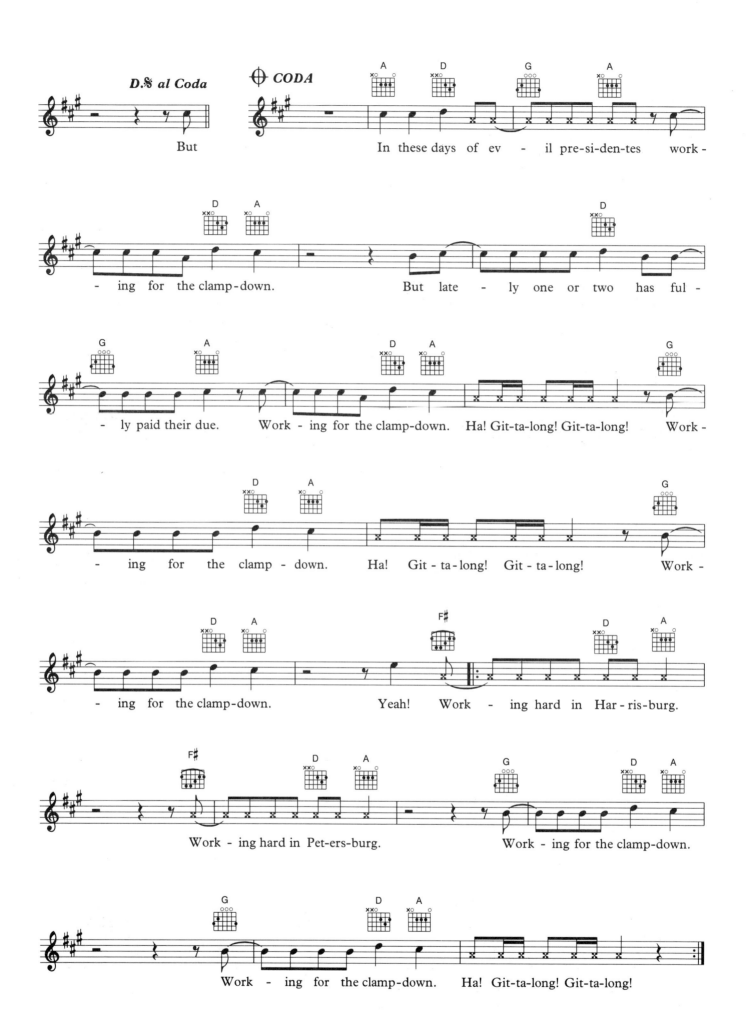

TRAIN IN VAIN

Words & Music by
Strummer/Jones

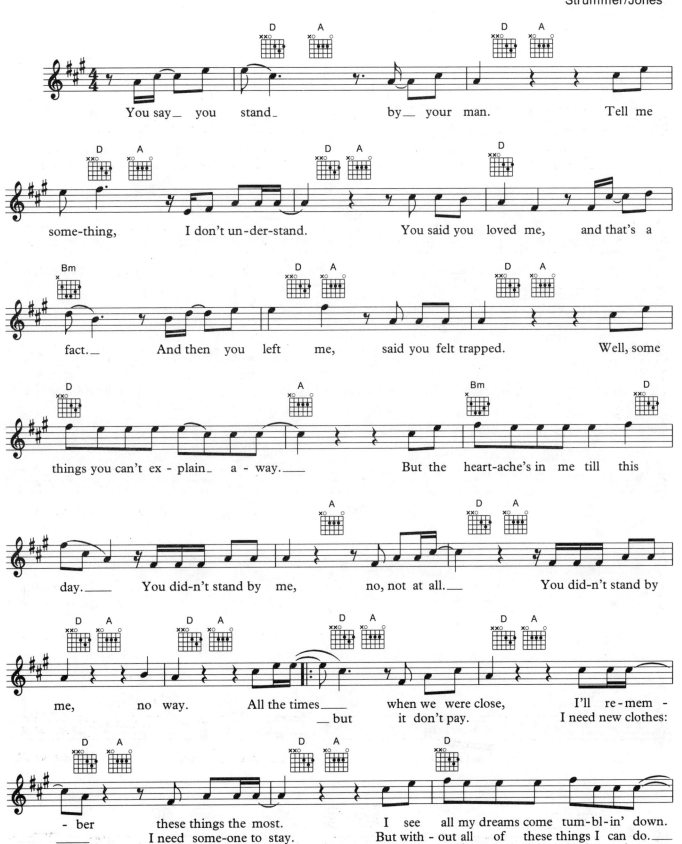

GUNS OF BRIXTON

Words & Music by
Paul Simonon

You . . . . When they

kick at   your front door   how you gon-na   come?   With your hands on your head   or on the

trig-ger   of your gun.   You can

crush us   you can bruise us   and ev-en shoot us   but   oh   the guns of

Brix-ton.   Shot down on the   pave-ment   wait-ing   in   death row,   his

game was sur-vi - vin' as in   hea-ven as   in hell. You can   crush us   you can bruise us   but you'll

have to an-swer to   oh   the guns of   Brix-ton.

SOMEBODY GOT MURDERED

Words & Music by
The Clash

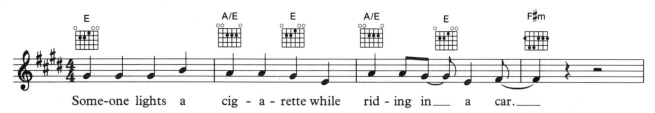

Some-one lights a cig-a-rette while rid-ing in a car.

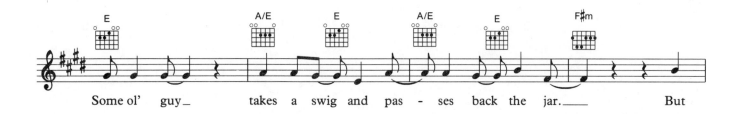

Some ol' guy takes a swig and pas-ses back the jar. But

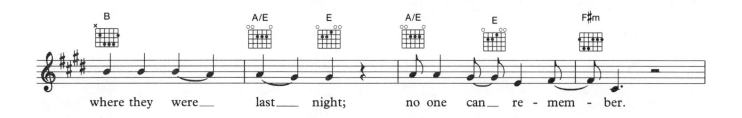

where they were last night; no one can re-mem-ber.

Some-bo-dy got mur-dered. Good-bye for keeps, for-ev-er.

Some-bo-dy got mur-dered.

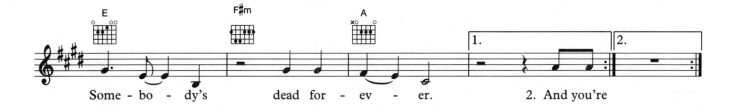

Some-bo-dy's dead for-ev-er. 2. And you're

21

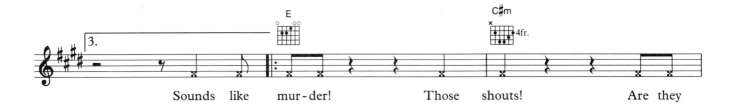

Sounds like mur-der! Those shouts! Are they

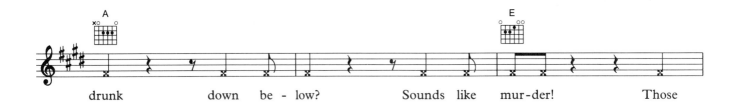

drunk down be - low? Sounds like mur-der! Those

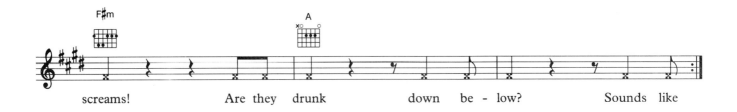

screams! Are they drunk down be - low? Sounds like

2. And you're minding your own business,
   Carrying spare change.
   You wouldn't cosh a barber.
   You're hungry all the same.
   I been very tempted
   To grab it from the till.
   I been very hungry
   But not enough to kill.

   Somebody got murdered
   Somebody's dead forever.

3. Somebody got murdered
   His name cannot be found
   A small stain on the pavement,
   They'll scrub it off the ground.
   As the daily crowd disperses
   No one says that much.
   Somebody got murdered
   And it left me with a touch.

   Somebody got murdered
   Somebody's dead forever.

LOST IN THE SUPERMARKET

Words & Music by
Strummer/Jones

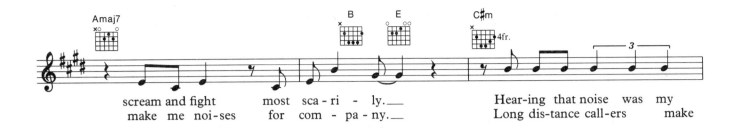

scream and fight most sca - ri - ly.___ Hear-ing that noise was my
make me noi-ses for com - pa - ny.___ Long dis-tance call-ers make

first ev - er feel - ing. That's how it's been all a - round me.
long dis - tance calls.___

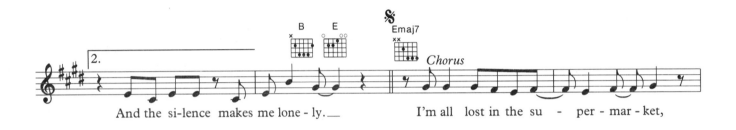

And the si-lence makes me lone - ly. ___ I'm all lost in the su - per - mar - ket,

I can no long-er shop hap - pi - ly._____ I came in here for that spe -

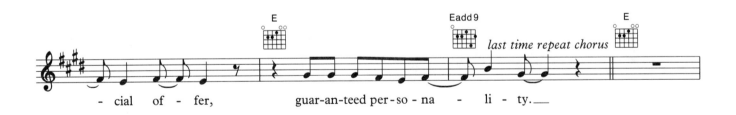

- cial of - fer, guar-an-teed per-so - na - li - ty. ___

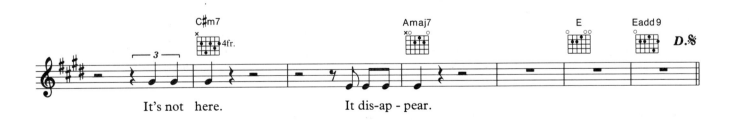

It's not here. It dis-ap - pear.

BANKROBBER

Words & Music by
Strummer/Jones

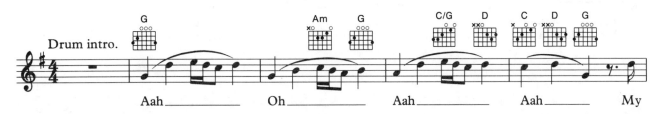

Aah_____ Oh_____ Aah_____ Aah_____ My

dad - dy was_____ a bank rob - ber but he ne - ver hurt_ no - bo - dy.

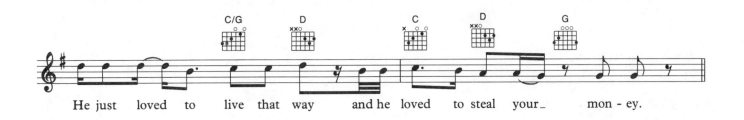

He just loved to live that way and he loved to steal your_ mon - ey.

Some is rich_ and some is poor, that's the way_ the world is. But I
old man spoke up in a bar,_ said I ne - ver been to pri - son.

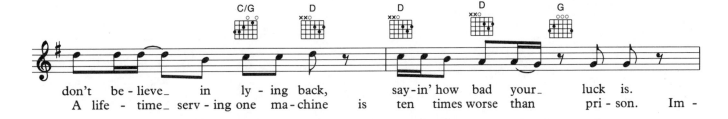

don't be - lieve_ in ly - ing back, say-in' how bad your_ luck is.
A life - time_ serv - ing one ma - chine is ten times worse than pri - son. Im -

So we came to jazz it up, we ne - ver loved a sho - vel.
-a-gine if all the boys in jail could get out now_ to - ge - ther.

Break your back to earn your pay, and don't for-get to gro - vel.
Whad-da you think they'd want to say to us while we was be - ing cle - ver?

Dad - dy was a bank rob - ber but he ne - ver hurt no - bo - dy.
Some day you'll meet your rock-ing chair 'cos that's where we're spin - ning.

He just loved to live that way and he loved to take our_ mon - ey.
There's no point to wan-na comb your hair, when it's grey and thin-ning.

Aah Oh Aah Aah Aah
Aah Oh Aah Aah Aah

Oh Aah Oh The Oh
Oh Aah

Dad - dy was a bank rob - ber but he ne - ver hurt_ no - bo - dy.

He just loved to live that way and he loved to steal your_ mon - ey.

So we came to jazz it up,_ we ne - ver loved a sho - vel.

26

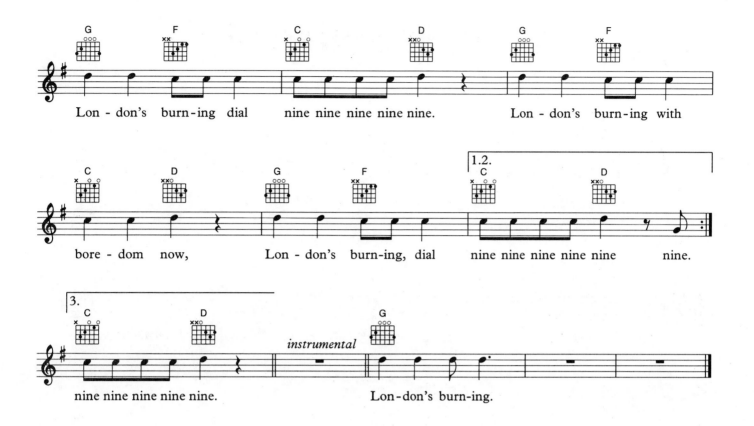

Lon-don's burn-ing dial nine nine nine nine nine. Lon-don's burn-ing with

bore-dom now, Lon-don's burn-ing, dial nine nine nine nine nine nine.

1.2.

3.

instrumental

nine nine nine nine nine. Lon-don's burn-ing.

JANIE JONES

Words & Music by
Strummer/Jones

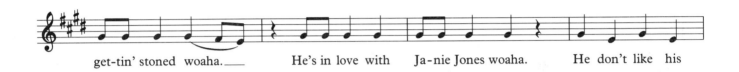

He's in love with rock 'n roll woaha._____ He's in love with

get-tin' stoned woaha._____ He's in love with Ja-nie Jones woaha. He don't like his

bor-ing job no. He's in love with rock 'n roll woaha._ He's in love with

get-tin' stoned woaha._____ He's in love with Ja-nie Jones woaha. He don't like his

4th time **to Coda** ⊕

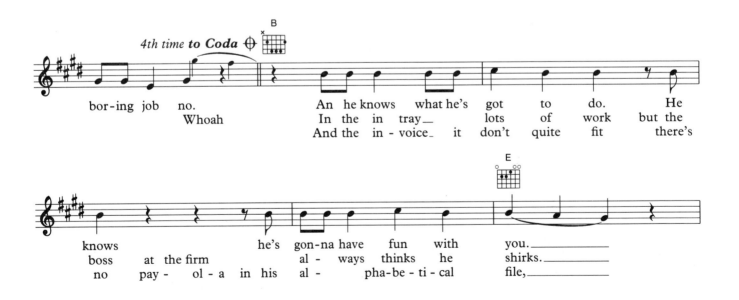

bor-ing job no. An he knows what he's got to do. He
Whoah In the in tray_ lots of work but the
And the in - voice_ it don't quite fit there's

knows he's gon-na have fun with you._____
boss at the firm al - ways thinks he shirks._____
no pay - ol - a in his al - pha-be-ti-cal file,_____

You luck-y la - dy.

'cept for the go-vern-ment man

An' he knows when the eve - ning comes, when his
But he's just like ev' - ry one he's got a
this time he's gon - na real - ly tell the boss he's gon - na

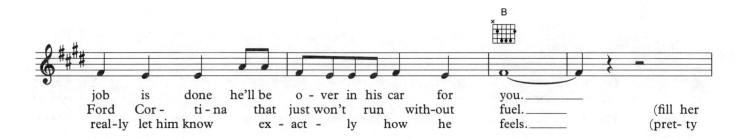

job is done he'll be o - ver in his car for you.____
Ford Cor - ti - na that just won't run with-out fuel.____ (fill her
real-ly let him know ex - act - ly how he feels.____ (pret- ty

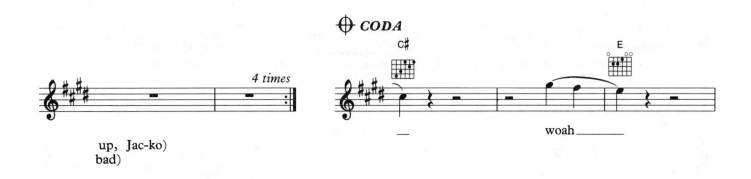

4 times

⊕ *CODA*

woah____

up, Jac-ko)
bad)

woah.____ Let them know.____ Let them know.____

33

TOMMY GUN

Words & Music by
Strummer/Jones

Tom - my gun _____ a - you ain't hap-py 'less you've got one.

Tom - my gun _____ ain't gon-na shoot the place up _____ just for fun. May -

- be he wants to die for the mon - ey. _____ May - be he wants to kill

for his coun - try. What - ev - er he wants he's gon - na get it.

O K   so let's ag-ree   a-bout the price.

Boats an' tanks an' planes   it's your   game.

Kings an' queens an'   gen-er-als   learn-ing your name._   I   seen all   of the

in - no - cents   the hu-man sac-ri - fice._____   If   death comes   so

cheap   then the   same   goes   for   life._____

2. Tommy gun
   You better strip it down for a customs run.
   Tommy gun
   Waiting at the airport 'til kingdom come,
   And we can watch you make it on the nine o'clock news.
   Standing there in Palestine
   Lighting the fuse.
   Whatever you want you're gonna get it.

   Tommy gun, tommy gun.

3. Tommy gun
   You'll be dead when the war is won.
   Tommy gun
   But did you have to gun down everyone?
   I can see it's kill or be killed,
   A nation of destiny has gotta be fulfilled.
   Whatever you want you're gonna get it.

4. Tommy gun
   You can be a hero in an age of none.
   Tommy gun
   I'm cutting out your picture from page one.
   I'm gonna get a jacket just like yours
   An' give my false support to your cause.
   Whatever you want you're gonna get it.
   Alright.

COMPLETE CONTROL

Words & Music by
Strummer/Jones

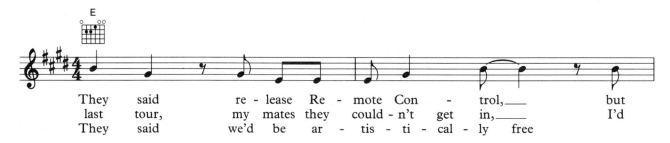

They said   re - lease Re - mote Con - trol,____   but
last   tour,   my mates they could - n't get in,____   I'd
They said   we'd be ar - tis - ti - cal - ly free

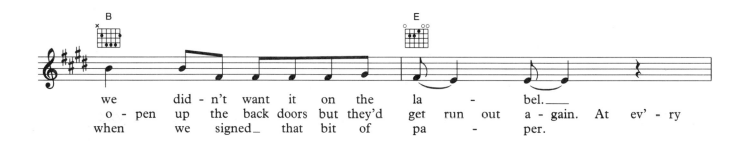

we   did - n't want it on the la - bel.____ At ev' - ry
o - pen up the back doors but they'd get run out a - gain. At ev' - ry
when   we signed_ that bit of pa - per.

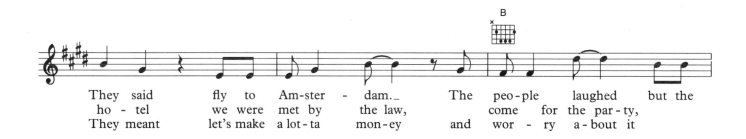

They said   fly to Am - ster - dam._ The peo - ple laughed but the
ho - tel   we were met by the law,   come for the par - ty,
They meant let's make a lot - ta mon - ey and wor - ry a - bout it

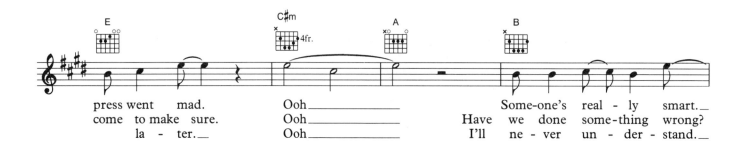

press went mad.   Ooh____   Some - one's real - ly smart._
come to make sure.   Ooh____   Have we done some - thing wrong?
la - ter._   Ooh____   I'll ne - ver un - der - stand._

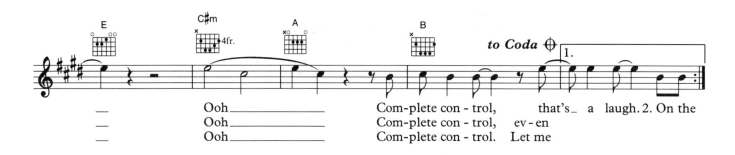

to Coda ⊕ |1.
____   Ooh____   Com - plete con - trol,   that's_ a laugh. 2. On the
____   Ooh____   Com - plete con - trol,   ev - en
____   Ooh____   Com - plete con - trol. Let me

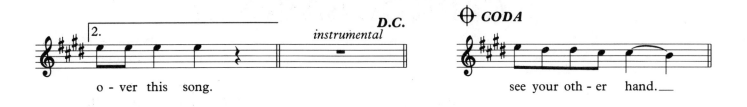

instrumental **D.C.**

o - ver this song.

⊕ CODA

see your oth - er hand.___

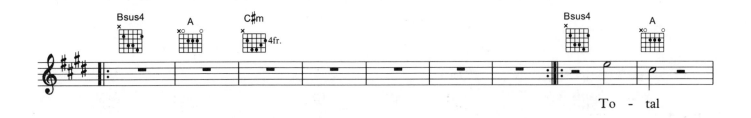

Bsus4　A　C#m　Bsus4　A

To - tal

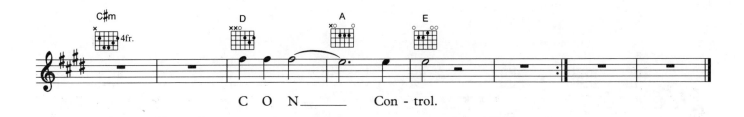

C#m　D　A　E

C O N_____ Con - trol.

I don't trust you
Why should you trust me, huh?
All over newspapers
They're filthy, they're dirty
They ain't gonna last
This Joe Public speaking
I'm controlled in the body
I'm controlled in the mind
This the punk rockers
Controlled by the price of
The first drugs we must find.

CAPITOL RADIO

Words & Music by
Strummer/Jones

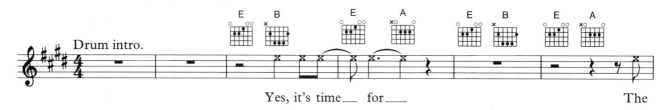

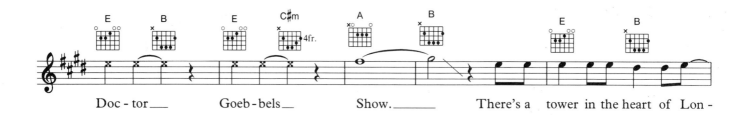

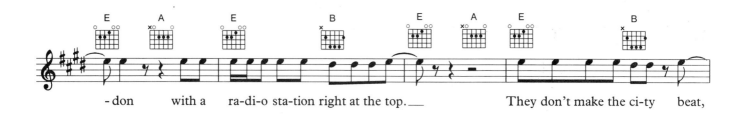

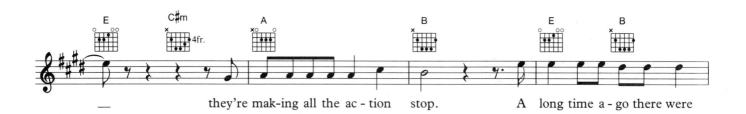

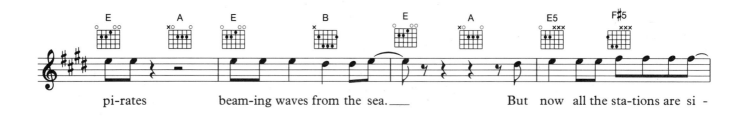

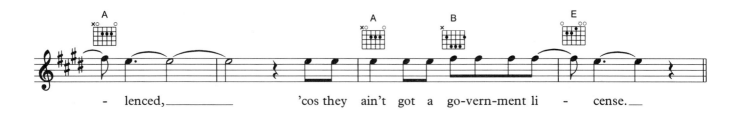

Yes, it's time___ for___ The Doc-tor___ Goeb-bels___ Show._____ There's a tower in the heart of Lon - -don with a ra-di-o sta-tion right at the top.___ They don't make the ci-ty beat, ___ they're mak-ing all the ac-tion stop. A long time a-go there were pi-rates beam-ing waves from the sea.___ But now all the sta-tions are si - -lenced,_____ 'cos they ain't got a go-vern-ment li - cense.___

Wan-na tell___ your prob - lems, phone in from your bed - sit room? Hav-ing

trou-ble with your part - ner? Let us all in on the news. If you

wan-na hear a re - cord get the word from Ai - den Day.___

He picks all the hits to play,_____ to keep you in your place all

day._____

Ca - pi - tol Ra - di - o,___
In tune with no-thing,

repeat 7 times ad lib.

ca - pi - tol ra - di - o.___ Don't touch that dial.
in___ tune with no-thing.

WHITE RIOT

Words & Music by
Strummer/Jones

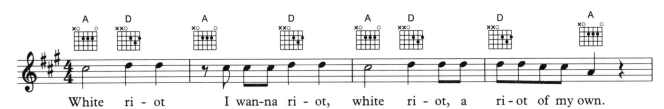

White ri - ot   I wan-na ri - ot, white ri - ot, a ri - ot of my own.

to Coda ⊕

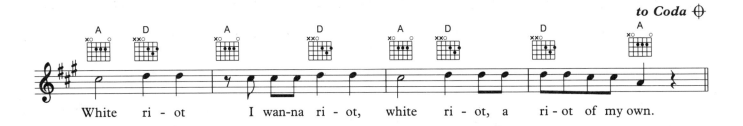

White ri - ot   I wan-na ri - ot, white ri - ot, a ri - ot of my own.

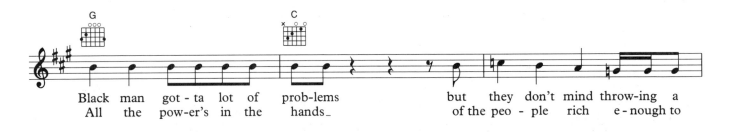

Black man got - ta lot of prob-lems   but they don't mind throw-ing a
All the pow-er's in the hands_   of the peo - ple rich e - nough to

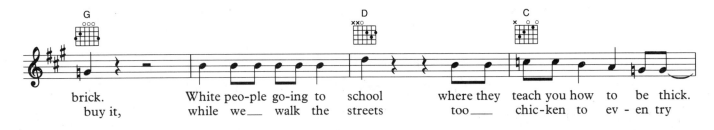

brick.   White peo-ple go-ing to school   where they teach you how to be thick.
buy it,   while we_ walk the streets   too_ chic-ken to ev - en try

_   An' ev'-ry-bo-dy's do-in'   just what they're told to
it.

D.C. al Coda
instrumental

and no-bo-dy wants   to go to jail.

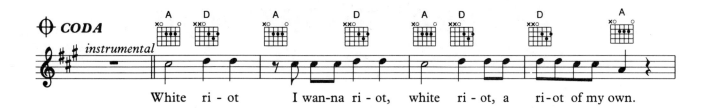

⊕ *CODA*

instrumental

White ri - ot   I wan-na ri - ot,   white ri - ot, a   ri-ot of my own.

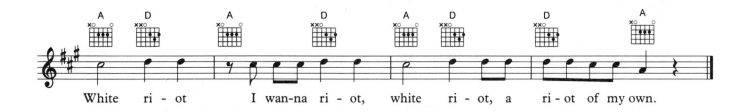

White ri - ot   I wan-na ri - ot,   white ri - ot, a   ri - ot of my own.

White riot, I wanna riot,
White riot, a riot of my own.

Black man got a lotta problems
But they don't mind throwing a brick
White people go to school
Where they teach you how to be thick

An' everybody's doing
Just what they're told to
An' nobody wants to go to jail

White riot, I wanna riot,
White riot, a riot of my own.

All the power is in the hands
Of people rich enough to buy it
While we walk the streets
Too chicken to even try it

An' everybody's doing
Just what they're told to
An' nobody wants to go to jail

Are you taking over
Or are you taking orders
Are you going backwards
Or are you going forwards

White riot, I wanna riot,
White riot, a riot of my own.
White riot, I wanna riot,
White riot, a riot of my own.

CAREER OPPORTUNITIES

Words & Music by
Strummer/Jones

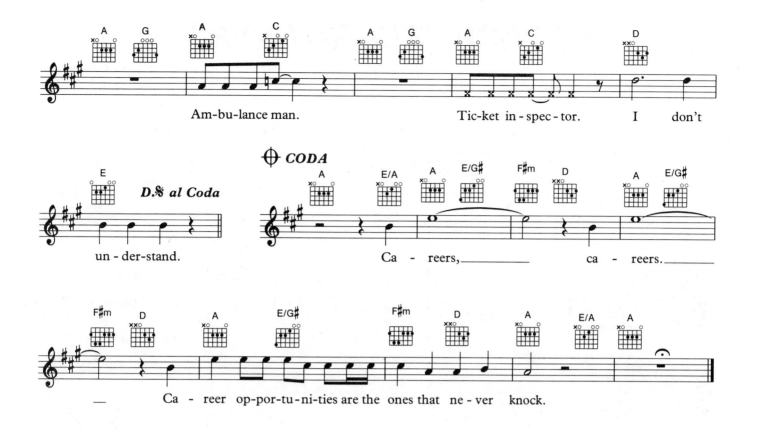

Am-bu-lance man.   Tic-ket in-spec-tor.   I   don't

CODA

D.% al Coda

un-der-stand.   Ca - reers,_____   ca - reers._____

—   Ca - reer op-por-tu-ni-ties are the ones that ne - ver   knock.

2. *(instrumental)*
   I hate all of my school's rules.
   They just think that I'm another fool.

   Career opportunities are the ones that never knock.
   Every job they offered you is to keep you out the dock.
   Career opportunities are the ones that never knock.

3. They're gonna have to introduce conscription.
   They're gonna have to take away my prescription.
   If they wanna get me making toys,
   If they wanna get me, I got no choice.

   Career opportunities are the ones that never knock.
   Every job they offered you is to keep you out the dock.
   Career opportunities are the ones that never knock.

CLASH CITY ROCKERS

Words & Music by
Strummer/Jones

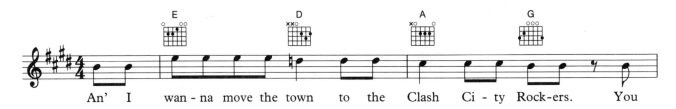

An' I wan-na move the town to the Clash Ci-ty Rock-ers. You

need a lit-tle jump of e-lec-tri-cal shock-ers. Bet-ter leave town if you

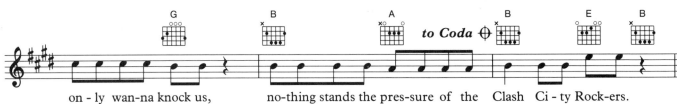

on-ly wan-na knock us, no-thing stands the pres-sure of the Clash Ci-ty Rock-ers.

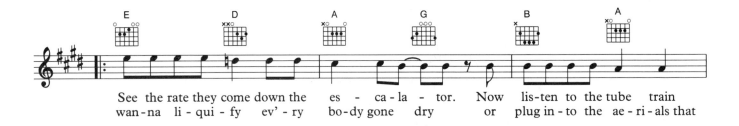

See the rate they come down the es-ca-la-tor. Now lis-ten to the tube train
wan-na li-qui-fy ev'-ry bo-dy gone dry or plug in-to the ae-ri-als that

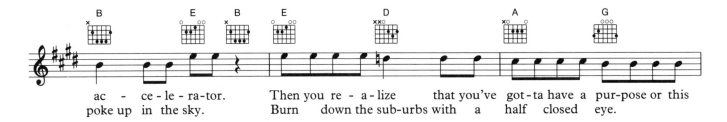

ac-ce-le-ra-tor. Then you re-a-lize that you've got-ta have a pur-pose or this
poke up in the sky. Burn down the sub-urbs with a half closed eye.

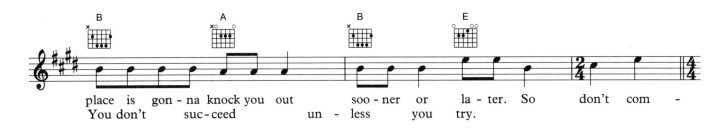

place is gon-na knock you out soo-ner or la-ter. So don't com -
You don't suc-ceed un-less you try.

44

-plain _____ a-bout your use-less em - ploy - ment, jack it in

for-ev-er to - night, _____ or shut your mouth _____ an' pre-tend to en -

-joy __ it. Think of all the mon-ey you got. An' I

Yeah yeah.   **D.C. al Coda**
instrumental

⊕ *CODA*

Clash Ci-ty Rock-ers. _____ You

owe me a move say the bells of Saint Groove. Come on and show me say the

bells of old Bow - ie. When I am fit - ter say the bells of Ga-ry Glit - ter. No

one but you and I _____ say the bells of Prince Far I. No one but you and I __

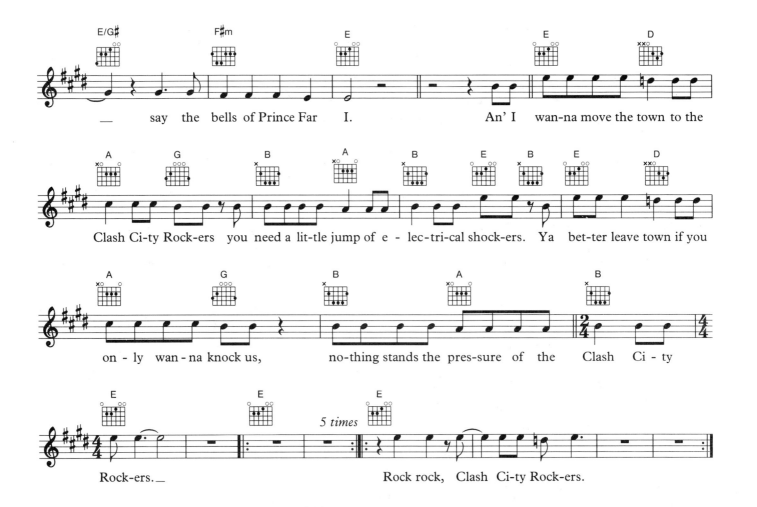

say the bells of Prince Far I.   An' I wan-na move the town to the

Clash Ci-ty Rock-ers you need a lit-tle jump of e - lec-tri-cal shock-ers. Ya bet-ter leave town if you

on - ly wan - na knock us,   no-thing stands the pres-sure of the   Clash   Ci - ty

Rock-ers. __   Rock rock, Clash Ci-ty Rock-ers.

5 times

An' I wanna move the town to the Clash City Rockers
Ya need a little jump of electrical shockers
Ya better leave town if you only wanna knock us
Nothing stands the pressure of the Clash City Rockers.

Ya see the rate they come down the escalator
Now listen to the tube train accelerator
Then you realise that you've got to have a purpose
Or this place is gonna knock you out sooner or later.

So don't complain about your useless employment
Jack it in forever tonight
Or shut your mouth an' pretend to enjoy it
Think of all the money you got.

An' I wanna liquify everybody gone dry
Or plug into the aerials that poke up in the sky
Or burn down the suburbs with a half closed eye
You don't succeed unless you try.

You owe me a move say the bells of Saint Groove
Come on and show me say the bells of old Bowie
When I am fitter say the bells of Gary Glitter
No one but you and I say the bells of prince Far I.

An' I wanna move the town to the Clash City Rockers
Ya need a little jump of electrical shockers
Ya better leave town if you only wanna knock us
Nothing stands the pressure of the Clash City Rockers.

Rock Rock – Clash City Rockers
Rock Rock – Clash City Rockers

SAFE EUROPEAN HOME

Words & Music by
Strummer/Jones

Well, I just got back_ an' I wish I ne-ver leave now. (Where d'ya go?)_

_ Who dat Mar - tian ar - ri - val at_ the air - port, yeah? (Where d'ya go?)

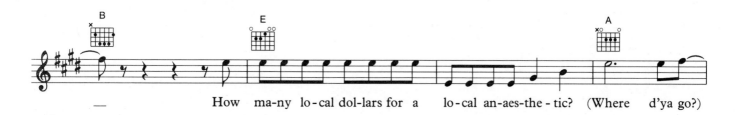

_ How ma-ny lo-cal dol-lars for a lo-cal an-aes-the - tic? (Where d'ya go?)

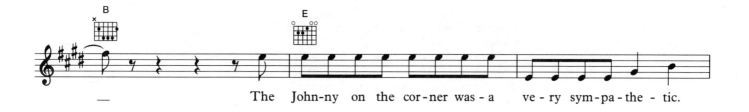

_ The John-ny on the cor-ner was - a ve - ry sym-pa-the - tic.

(Where d'ya go?)___ I went to the place where ev-'ry white face is an

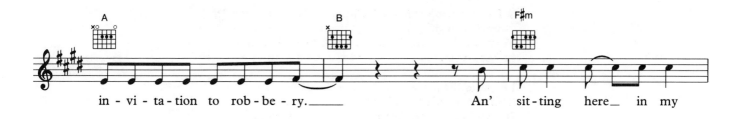

in - vi - ta-tion to rob-be - ry.___ An' sit-ting here_ in my

safe Eu-ro-pe - an home, don't wan-na go-back there a - gain.

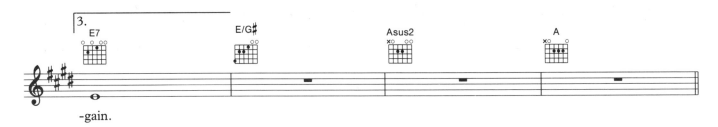

-gain.

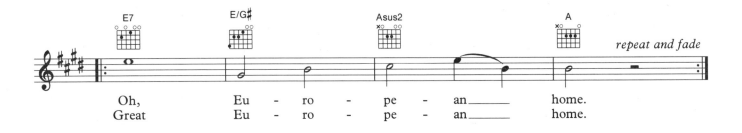

repeat and fade

Oh, Eu - ro - pe - an_____ home.
Great Eu - ro - pe - an_____ home.

2. Wasn't I lucky an' wouldn't it be loverly?
   (Where d'ya go?)
   Send us all cards, have a laying in on Sunday.
   (Where d'ya go?)
   I was there for two weeks, so how come I never tell now?
   (Where d'ya go?)
   That natty dread drink in the Sheraton Hotel, yeah.
   (Where d'ya go?)

   I went to the place
   Where ev'ry white face
   Is an invitation to robbery.
   An' sitting here
   In my safe European home,
   Don't wanna go back there again.

3. They got the sun, they got the palm trees.
   (Where d'ya go?)
   They got the weed, they got the taxis.
   (Where d'ya go?)
   Whoa, the harder they come, the home of ol' Blue Beat.
   (Where d'ya go?)
   I'd stay an' be a tourist, but I can't take the gun play.
   (Where d'ya go?)

   I went to the place
   Where ev'ry white face
   Is an invitation to robbery.
   An' sitting here
   In my safe European home,
   Don't wanna go back there again.

STAY FREE

Words & Music by
Strummer/Jones

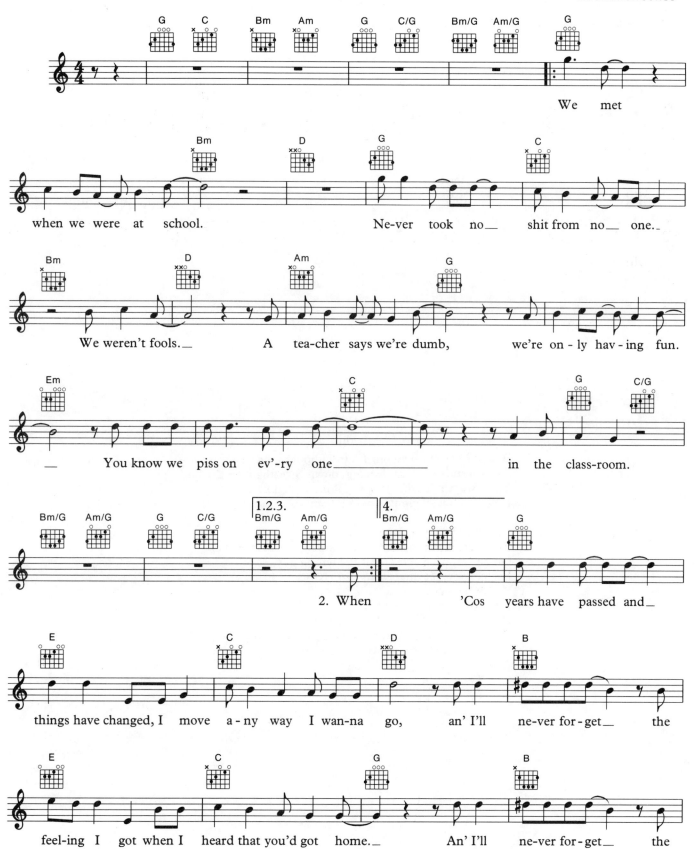

smile on my face 'cos I knew where you would be.____ An' if you're in__ the__

Crown to-night have a drink on me,____ but go ea - sy, step

light - ly, stay free.

2. When we got thrown out I left without much fuss
   At weekends we'd go dancing, down Streatham on the bus,
   You always made me laugh, got me in bad fights,
   Play me pool all night, smokin' menthol.

3. I practised daily in my room,
   You were down the Crown planning your next move,
   Go on a nicking spree – hit the wrong guy.
   Each of you get three years in Brixton.

4. I did my very best to write,
   How was Butlins, were the screws too tight?
   When you lot get out we're gonna hit the town,
   We'll burn it fuckin' down to a cinder.

SPANISH BOMBS

Words & Music by
Strummer/Jones

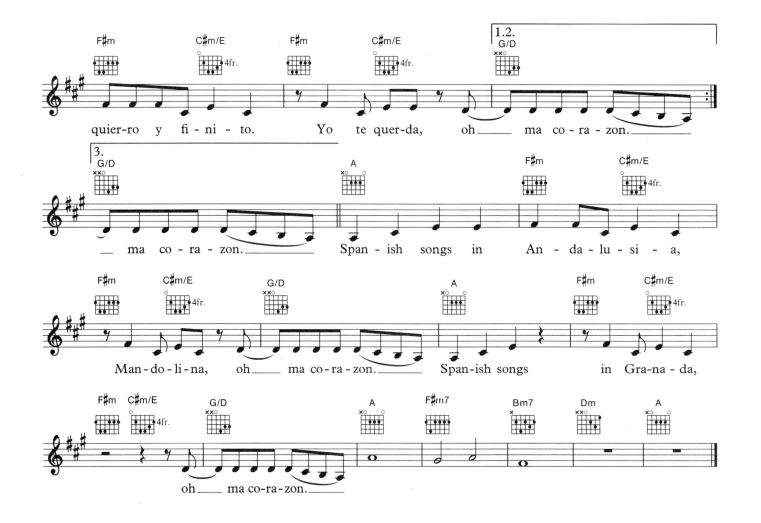

quier-ro y fi - ni - to. Yo te quer-da, oh___ ma co - ra - zon.___

__ ma co - ra - zon.___ Span - ish songs in An - da - lu - si - a,

Man - do - li - na, oh___ ma co - ra - zon.___ Span-ish songs in Gra - na - da,

oh___ ma co-ra-zon.___

2. Spanish weeks in my disco casino,
   The freedom fighters died up on the hill.
   They sang the red flag, they wore the black one,
   But after they died it was Mockingbird Hill.
   Back home the buses went up in flashes
   The Irish tomb was drenched in blood.
   Spanish bombs shatter the hotels.
   My señorita's rose was nipped in the bud.

   Spanish bombs, yo te quierro y finito.
   Yo te querda, oh ma corazon.
   Spanish bombs, yo te quierro y finito.
   Yo te querda, oh ma corazon.

3. The hillsides ring with 'Free the people'
   Or can I hear the echo from the days of '39?
   With trenches full of poets, the ragged army
   Fixin' bayonets to fight the other line,
   Spanish bombs rock the province.
   I'm hearing music from another time.
   Spanish bombs on the Costa Brava,
   I'm flying in on a DC-10 tonight.

   Spanish bombs, yo te quierro y finito.
   Yo te querda, oh ma corazon.
   Spanish bombs, yo te quierro y finito.
   Yo te querda, oh ma corazon.

ENGLISH CIVIL WAR

Words & Music
Traditional
Arr. Strummer/Jones

When John-ny comes march-ing home a-gain, Hur -
- rah   Tra - la.   He's com-ing by bus or un - der-ground, Hur -
- rah   Tra - la.   The wom-an's eye_ will shed a tear to see his face_ so
bea-ten in fear.   Just a-round the cor-ner in the Eng-lish ci-vil war.__

2. Still at the stage of clubs and fists,
Hurrah. Tra la.
When that well known face got beaten to bits,
Hurrah. Tra la.
Your face was blue in the light of the screen
As we watched the speech of an animal scream,
The new party army was marching right over our heads,
Alright.

3. There they are, Ha Ha, I told you so.
Tra la.
Hurrah says everybody that we know.
Hurrah. Tra la.
But who hid a radio under the stairs?
An' who got caught out on their unawares?
When that new party army came marching right up the stairs.

4. When Johnny comes marching home again,
Hurrah. Tra la.
Nobody understands it could happen again,
Hurrah. Tra la.
The sun is shining and the kids are shouting loud,
You gotta know it's shining through a crack in the cloud.
The shadows keep on falling when Johnny comes marching home,
Alright.

Johnny, OK. Johnny, all the girls go Whoah,
Get his coffin ready, cos Johnny's comin' home.